DETROIT PUBLIC LIBRARY

910.9141
J M323s

P9-CRW-639
3 5674 03986990 5

Rookie

Read-About® Geography

The Seven Continents

By Wil Mara

Consultant
Nanci R. Vargus, Ed.D.
Assistant Professor of Literacy
University of Indianapolis, Indianapolis, Indiana

Children's Press®
A Division of Scholastic Inc.
New York   Toronto   London   Auckland   Sydney
Mexico City   New Delhi   Hong Kong
Danbury, Connecticut

Designer: Herman Adler Design
Photo Researcher: Caroline Anderson
The photo on the cover shows North America, South America, Europe,
Asia, Australia, Africa, and Antarctica.

Library of Congress Cataloging-in-Publication Data

Mara, Wil.
  The seven continents / by Wil Mara.— 1st ed.
    p. cm. — (Rookie read-about geography)
  Includes index.
  ISBN 0-516-22748-3 (lib. bdg.)   0-516-22534-0 (pbk.)
  1. Continents—Juvenile literature. I. Title. II. Series.
  G133.M343 2005
  910'.914'1—dc22
                                    2004015575

©2005 by Scholastic Inc.
All rights reserved. Published simultaneously in Canada.
Printed in the United States of America.

CHILDREN'S PRESS, and ROOKIE READ-ABOUT®,
and associated logos are trademarks and or registered trademarks
of Scholastic Library Publishing. SCHOLASTIC and associated logos
are trademarks and or registered trademarks of Scholastic Inc.
1 2 3 4 5 6 7 8 9 10 R 14 13 12 11 10 09 08 07 06 05

Do you know you live on a continent?

This is the continent of North America.

Imagine you are on a spaceship. You are looking down at Earth. You would see land and water.

The largest pieces of land are continents.

Do you see land in this picture?

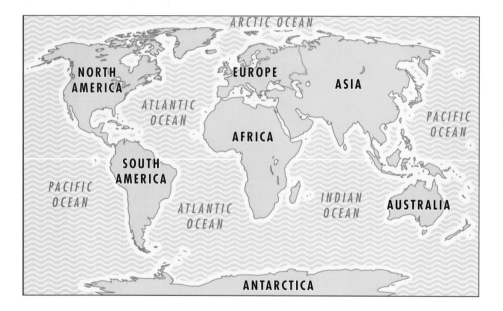

ARCTIC OCEAN

NORTH AMERICA

EUROPE

ASIA

ATLANTIC OCEAN

PACIFIC OCEAN

AFRICA

SOUTH AMERICA

PACIFIC OCEAN

ATLANTIC OCEAN

INDIAN OCEAN

AUSTRALIA

ANTARCTICA

There are seven continents in the world. They are Asia, Africa, North America, South America, Europe, Antarctica, and Australia.

Asia is the largest continent.

There are many countries
in Asia. China, Japan, Israel,
India, and part of Russia
are in Asia.

More than three billion
people live in Asia!

Over eight million people live in Tokyo, Japan.

These men are riding across the Sahara Desert.

Africa is the second-largest continent.

Egypt, Ghana, South Africa, and many other countries are in Africa.

The world's largest desert is in Africa. It is called the Sahara Desert.

North America is the third-largest continent.

Canada, the United States, Mexico, Bermuda, and Panama are all part of North America.

You can see buildings like these in many North American cities.

This is Seattle, Washington.

This rain forest is in Peru.

South America is the fourth-largest continent.

Brazil, Argentina, and Peru are countries you can visit in South America.

There are many tropical rain forests in South America.

Europe is a continent near Asia and Africa.

Germany, Italy, England, Spain, part of Russia, and France are all in Europe.

Europe has many landmarks.

The Eiffel Tower in Paris, France, is one landmark in Europe.

These penguins live in Antarctica.

Antarctica surrounds the South Pole. It is the coldest continent.

Temperatures there can be -20°F (-29°C) in the summer!

Australia is the smallest continent.

Some of the land there is flat and rocky. It is good for raising sheep and cattle.

Some ranchers raise sheep in Australia.

Some large islands look like continents, but they are not. Each one is part of the continent closest to it.

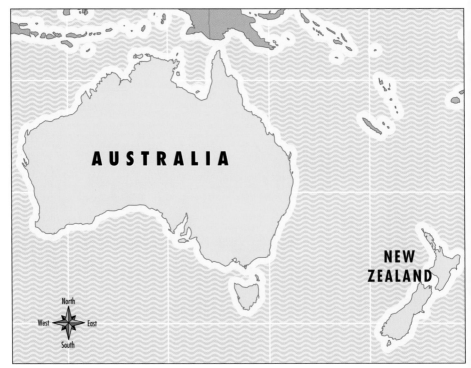

New Zealand is part of Australia.

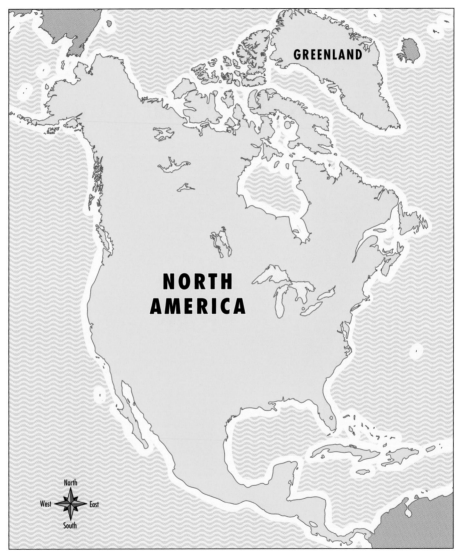

Greenland is part of North America.

Scientists think that long ago there was only one continent.

This continent was very big. Then it broke into smaller pieces. The pieces moved apart.

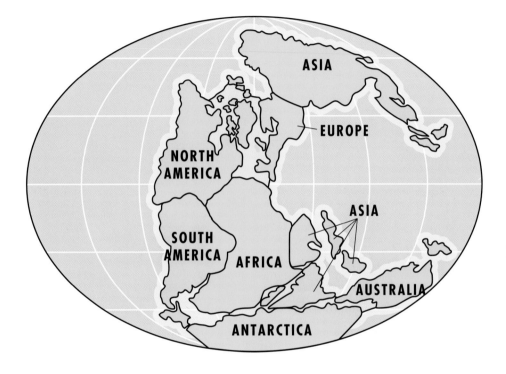

The continents are still moving today. They are moving too slow for us to feel or see.

What continent are you on? Be still. Can you feel it moving?

Which continent would you like to visit?

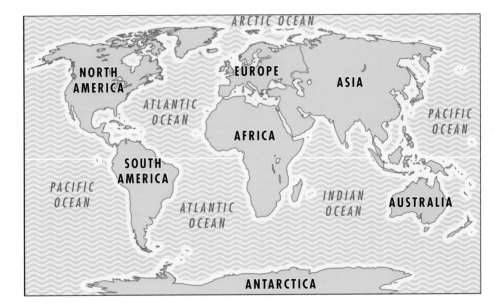

29

Words You Know

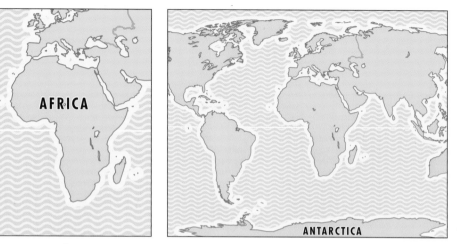

Africa

Antarctica

Asia

Australia

Europe

North America

South America

31

Index

About the Author

Wil Mara is a writer who loves geography. He studies continents, countries, and islands. He also travels whenever he can. Wil recently visited Cuba (in North America) and plans to visit Europe next year.

Photo Credits

Photographs © 2005: Corbis Images: 26 (John Henley), 13 (Lester Lefkowitz), 17 (Royalty-Free), cover (Tom Van Sant); NASA: 5; The Image Works: 14 (Michael J. Doolittle), 9 (Fujifotos), 18 (Topham); Visuals Unlimited: 10 (Les Christman), 21 (S.K. Patrick), 3 (Hugh Rose).

Maps by Bob Italiano